T0144940

Printed in the USA
CPSIA information can be obtained
at www.ICGtesting.com
JSHW072020140824
68134JS00040B/3711

9 780874 418767

סִדּוּר מַה-טּוֹב

A Family Shabbat Prayer Book
Conservative Edition

Text by Rabbi Lauren Kurland and Julie Schwartz Wohl

Illustrations by Julie Schwartz Wohl

Editorial Committee:
Rabbi Sharon Brous
Rabbi Nina Beth Cardin
Rabbi Martin S. Cohen
Rabbi Stuart Seltzer
Rabbi David Wolpe

Behrman House, Inc.

A Note on Transliteration:

We offer transliteration as a tool for not-yet-Hebrew readers to be able to participate more fully in the service. In our prayer book, *ch* corresponds to the Hebrew letters כ and ח.

Acknowledgments

Todah rabbah to the children, parents, and leaders of Ansche Chesed's Minyan Yigdal for piloting this siddur and helping to shape it to become a joyful, educational, and spiritual work. *Todah rabbah* to Lori Cohen and Chris Rothko for spearheading and generously sponsoring the Ansche Chesed printing of the pilot siddur. *Todah rabbah* to Rabbi Jeremy Kalmanofsky and Rabbi Stuart Seltzer for their thoughtful and careful edits.

—Rabbi Lauren Kurland and Julie Schwartz Wohl

Design: Stacey May
Project Editor: Terry S. Kaye
Copyright ©2010 by Behrman House, Inc.
Springfield, New Jersey
www.behrmanhouse.com

Library of Congress Cataloging-in-Publication Data

Siddur (Reform). English & Hebrew.
    Siddur Mah Tov : a family Shabbat prayer book / text by Lauren Kurland and Julie Schwartz Wohl; illustrations by Julie Schwartz Wohl.
        p. cm.
    ISBN 978-0-87441-875-0 (conservative hardcover) -- ISBN 978-0-87441-855-2 (reform hard cover) -- ISBN 978-0-87441-876-7 (conservative paperback) -- ISBN 978-0-87441-856-9 (reform paperback)
1. Siddurim--Texts. 2. Reform Judaism--Liturgy--Texts. I. Kurland, Lauren. II. Wohl, Julie Schwartz. III. Title.
    BM674.34.K87 2010
    296.4'5046--dc22

                                        2009049540

A Note to Families

Prayer has brought us together as a community this Shabbat morning. We arrive as a family, and we participate as individuals as we each seek our own meaning from the words and melodies.

Siddur Mah Tov will add a new dimension to each person's worship experience—it adds the visual and emotional resonance of art to the traditional words of the service. Each original painting is a visual interpretation of one of our morning prayers. Perhaps it will inspire you to think in new terms about what the words mean to you, to create your own mental prayer images, and to share your vision with your family.

So, take in the images. Consider them. Perhaps close your eyes for a moment, then look at them again. Take pleasure in the imagery and your feelings. With your child, ask: What do I see? What other images might I choose to express my interpretation of the prayer? How does the image—and how does the prayer—make me feel? And how do those feelings affect my personal experience of the prayer service at that moment?

May *Siddur Mah Tov* enhance your Shabbat in a dynamic, spiritually meaningful, and creative way.

Modeh/Modah Ani ✎ מוֹדֶה/מוֹדָה אֲנִי

מוֹדֶה/מוֹדָה
אֲנִי לְפָנֶיךָ,
מֶלֶךְ חַי וְקַיָּם,
שֶׁהֶחֱזַרְתָּ בִּי נִשְׁמָתִי בְּחֶמְלָה,
רַבָּה אֱמוּנָתֶךָ!

(Boys say) *Modeh* / (girls say) *Modah*
Ani l'fanecha,
Melech chai v'kayam,
Shehechezarta bi nishmati b'chemlah,
Rabah emunatecha!

Thank You God,
For taking care of my soul with love.
Thank You for allowing me to wake up this morning!

Mah Tovu ✺ מַה טֹבוּ

מַה טֹבוּ אֹהָלֶיךָ יַעֲקֹב, מִשְׁכְּנֹתֶיךָ יִשְׂרָאֵל!

Mah tovu ohalecha Ya'akov, mishk'notecha Yisrael!

Your tents are so good, O Jacob, and so are your homes, O Israel!

Hinei Mah-Tov ✺ הִנֵּה מַה-טוֹב

הִנֵּה מַה-טוֹב וּמַה-נָּעִים שֶׁבֶת אַחִים גַּם יָחַד.

Hinei mah-tov umah-na'im shevet achim gam yachad.

How wonderful it is when friends and family come together.

בִּרְכוֹת הַשַּׁחַר ⟽ Birchot Hashachar

בָּרוּךְ אַתָּה יְיָ אֱלֹהֵינוּ מֶלֶךְ הָעוֹלָם, אֲשֶׁר נָתַן לַשֶּׂכְוִי בִינָה לְהַבְחִין בֵּין יוֹם וּבֵין לָיְלָה.

Baruch Atah Adonai Eloheinu Melech ha'olam, asher natan lasechvi vinah l'havchin bein yom u'vein lailah.

Praised are You, God, Ruler of the universe, who makes us know the difference between day and night.

בָּרוּךְ אַתָּה יְיָ אֱלֹהֵינוּ מֶלֶךְ הָעוֹלָם, שֶׁעָשַׂנִי בְּצַלְמוֹ.

Baruch Atah Adonai Eloheinu Melech ha'olam, she'asani b'tzalmo.

Praised are You, God, Ruler of the universe, who made me in God's image.

בָּרוּךְ אַתָּה יְיָ אֱלֹהֵינוּ מֶלֶךְ הָעוֹלָם, שֶׁעָשַׂנִי בֶּן/בַּת חוֹרִין.

Baruch Atah Adonai Eloheinu Melech ha'olam, she'asani (boys say) *ben chorin* / (girls say) *bat chorin.*

Praised are You, God, Ruler of the universe, who made me free.

בָּרוּךְ אַתָּה יְיָ אֱלֹהֵינוּ מֶלֶךְ הָעוֹלָם, פּוֹקֵחַ עִוְרִים.

Baruch Atah Adonai Eloheinu Melech ha'olam, pokei'ach ivrim.

Praised are You, God, Ruler of the universe, who opens our eyes.

בָּרוּךְ אַתָּה יְיָ אֱלֹהֵינוּ מֶלֶךְ הָעוֹלָם, מַלְבִּישׁ עֲרֻמִּים.

Baruch Atah Adonai Eloheinu Melech ha'olam, malbish arumim.

Praised are You, God, Ruler of the universe, who clothes us.

בָּרוּךְ אַתָּה יְיָ אֱלֹהֵינוּ מֶלֶךְ הָעוֹלָם, שֶׁעָשָׂה לִי כָּל צָרְכִּי.

Baruch Atah Adonai Eloheinu Melech ha'olam, she'asah li kol tzorki.

Praised are You, God, Ruler of the universe, who provides for my every need.

בָּרוּךְ אַתָּה יְיָ אֱלֹהֵינוּ מֶלֶךְ הָעוֹלָם, הַמֵּכִין מִצְעֲדֵי גָבֶר.

Baruch Atah Adonai Eloheinu Melech ha-olam, hameichin mitz'adei gaver.

Praised are You, God, Ruler of the universe, who helps us move forward with strength.

הַלְלוּיָה!

הַלְלוּ אֵל בְּקָדְשׁוֹ, הַלְלוּהוּ בִּרְקִיעַ עֻזּוֹ.

הַלְלוּהוּ בִגְבוּרֹתָיו, הַלְלוּהוּ כְּרֹב גֻּדְלוֹ.

הַלְלוּהוּ בְּתֵקַע שׁוֹפָר, הַלְלוּהוּ בְּנֵבֶל וְכִנּוֹר.

הַלְלוּהוּ בְּתֹף וּמָחוֹל, הַלְלוּהוּ בְּמִנִּים וְעֻגָב.

הַלְלוּהוּ בְצִלְצְלֵי שָׁמַע, הַלְלוּהוּ בְּצִלְצְלֵי תְרוּעָה.

כֹּל הַנְּשָׁמָה תְּהַלֵּל יָהּ, הַלְלוּיָה!

Hal'luyah!
Hal'lu Eil b'kodsho, hal'luhu birki'a uzo.
Hal'luhu bigvurotav, hal'luhu k'rov gudlo.
Hal'luhu b'teika shofar, hal'luhu b'neivel v'chinor.
Hal'luhu b'tof umachol, hal'luhu b'minim v'ugav.
Hal'luhu b'tziltz'lei shama, hal'luhu b'tziltz'lei t'ru'ah.
Kol han'shamah t'haleil Yah, hal'luyah!

Halleluyah!
Praise God in the heavens; praise God in the world.
Praise God; tell of God's deeds, tell of God's greatness.
Praise God with the blowing of the shofar,
Praise God with harp and lyre.
Praise God with drum and dance,
Praise God with strings and flute.
Praise God with clashing cymbals,
Praise God with clanging cymbals.
Let every soul praise God, Halleluyah!

V'nomar Lefanav ⇝ וְנֹאמַר לְפָנָיו

וְנֹאמַר לְפָנָיו שִׁירָה חֲדָשָׁה, הַלְלוּיָה!

V'nomar l'fanav shirah chadashah, hal'luyah!

Let us sing a new song to God, Halleluyah!

Hal'lu-Hodu LaShem ⇝ הַלְלוּ-הוֹדוּ לַשֵּׁם

הַלְלוּ, הַלְלוּ, הַלְלוּ, הַלְלוּיָה,
הוֹדוּ לַשֵּׁם!

Hal'lu, hal'lu, hal'lu, hal'luyah,
Hodu laShem!

Praise God, Halleluyah,
Praise God!

Bar'chu ⤳ בָּרְכוּ

Leader:

בָּרְכוּ אֶת יְיָ הַמְבֹרָךְ!

Bar'chu et Adonai ham'vorach!

Praise God, the One who is blessed!

Congregation:

בָּרוּךְ יְיָ הַמְבֹרָךְ לְעוֹלָם וָעֶד!

Baruch Adonai ham'vorach l'olam va'ed!

Praised is God, the One who is blessed always and forever!

Leader:

בָּרוּךְ יְיָ הַמְבֹרָךְ לְעוֹלָם וָעֶד!

Baruch Adonai ham'vorach l'olam va'ed!

Praised is God, the One who is blessed always and forever!

Yotzeir Or ✒ יוֹצֵר אוֹר

בָּרוּךְ אַתָּה יְיָ אֱלֹהֵינוּ מֶלֶךְ הָעוֹלָם,
יוֹצֵר אוֹר וּבוֹרֵא חֹשֶךְ,
עֹשֶׂה שָׁלוֹם וּבוֹרֵא אֶת הַכֹּל.

Baruch Atah Adonai Eloheinu Melech ha'olam,
Yotzeir or uvorei choshech,
Oseh shalom uvorei et hakol.

Praised are You, God, Ruler of the universe,
You make light and create darkness,
You make peace and create everything.

Ahavah Rabah ‍ אַהֲבָה רַבָּה

אַהֲבָה רַבָּה אֲהַבְתָּנוּ, יְיָ אֱלֹהֵינוּ, חֶמְלָה גְדוֹלָה וִיתֵרָה חָמַלְתָּ עָלֵינוּ. אָבִינוּ מַלְכֵּנוּ, בַּעֲבוּר אֲבוֹתֵינוּ שֶׁבָּטְחוּ בְךָ. וַתְּלַמְּדֵם חֻקֵּי חַיִּים, כֵּן תְּחָנֵּנוּ וּתְלַמְּדֵנוּ, אָבִינוּ, הָאָב הָרַחֲמָן, הַמְרַחֵם, רַחֵם עָלֵינוּ. וְתֵן בְּלִבֵּנוּ לְהָבִין וּלְהַשְׂכִּיל, לִשְׁמֹעַ, לִלְמֹד וּלְלַמֵּד, לִשְׁמֹר וְלַעֲשׂוֹת וּלְקַיֵּם אֶת כָּל דִּבְרֵי תַלְמוּד תּוֹרָתֶךָ בְּאַהֲבָה.

Ahavah rabah ahavtanu, Adonai Eloheinu, chemlah g'dolah viteirah chamalta aleinu. Avinu Malkeinu, ba'avur avoteinu, shebat'chu v'cha. Vat'lam'deim chukei chayim, kein t'choneinu utlam'deinu, Avinu, ha'av harachaman, ham'racheim, racheim aleinu. V'tein b'libeinu l'havin ul'haskil, lishmo'a, lilmod ul'lameid, lishmor v'la'asot ul'kayeim et kol divrei talmud Toratecha b'ahavah.

God, Your love for us is great; Your caring for us has no end. As You taught our ancestors who placed their trust in You, please help us understand Your rules for living. Have compassion on us. Help us to understand, listen, learn and teach, and to follow all the words of Your Torah with love.

וְהָאֵר עֵינֵינוּ בְּתוֹרָתֶךָ, וְדַבֵּק לִבֵּנוּ בְּמִצְוֹתֶיךָ, וְיַחֵד לְבָבֵנוּ לְאַהֲבָה וּלְיִרְאָה אֶת שְׁמֶךָ. וְלֹא נֵבוֹשׁ לְעוֹלָם וָעֶד. כִּי בְשֵׁם קָדְשְׁךָ הַגָּדוֹל וְהַנּוֹרָא בָּטָחְנוּ, נָגִילָה וְנִשְׂמְחָה בִּישׁוּעָתֶךָ.

V'ha'eir eineinu b'Toratecha, v'dabeik libeinu b'mitzvotecha, v'yacheid l'vaveinu l'ahavah ul'yir'ah et sh'mecha. V'lo neivosh l'olam va'ed. Ki v'sheim kodsh'cha hagadol v'hanora batachnu, nagilah v'nism'chah biyshu'atecha.

Brighten our eyes with Your Torah and connect our hearts to Your mitzvot with love and wonder, and may we never feel shame. We trust in Your awesome name, and we will celebrate and be glad because You take care of us.

וַהֲבִיאֵנוּ לְשָׁלוֹם מֵאַרְבַּע כַּנְפוֹת הָאָרֶץ, וְתוֹלִיכֵנוּ קוֹמְמִיּוּת לְאַרְצֵנוּ, כִּי אֵל פּוֹעֵל יְשׁוּעוֹת אָתָּה, וּבָנוּ בָחַרְתָּ מִכָּל עַם וְלָשׁוֹן. וְקֵרַבְתָּנוּ לְשִׁמְךָ הַגָּדוֹל סֶלָה בֶּאֱמֶת, לְהוֹדוֹת לְךָ וּלְיַחֶדְךָ בְּאַהֲבָה. בָּרוּךְ אַתָּה יְיָ, הַבּוֹחֵר בְּעַמּוֹ יִשְׂרָאֵל בְּאַהֲבָה.

Vahavi'einu l'shalom mei'arba kanfot ha'aretz, v'tolicheinu kom'miyut l'artzeinu, ki Eil po'eil y'shu'ot Atah, uvanu vacharta mikol-am v'lashon. V'keiravtanu l'shimcha hagadol selah be'emet, l'hodot l'cha ul'yachedcha b'ahavah. Baruch Atah Adonai, habocheir b'amo Yisrael b'ahavah.

Bring us together in peace from the four corners of the earth. Lead us to our land. You are a powerful God who has made us unique among all people on earth. Bring us closer to You so we may praise You with love. Praised are You, God, who, with love, has made the people Israel unique.

Sh'ma ✏ שְׁמַע

שְׁמַע יִשְׂרָאֵל, יְיָ אֱלֹהֵינוּ, יְיָ אֶחָד.

Sh'ma Yisrael, Adonai Eloheinu, Adonai Echad.

Hear O Israel, Adonai is our God, Adonai is One.

בָּרוּךְ שֵׁם כְּבוֹד מַלְכוּתוֹ לְעוֹלָם וָעֶד.

Baruch sheim k'vod malchuto l'olam va'ed.

Praised is God, for God is with us always and forever.

V'ahavta ⤶ וְאָהַבְתָּ

וְאָהַבְתָּ אֵת יְיָ אֱלֹהֶיךָ בְּכָל-לְבָבְךָ וּבְכָל-נַפְשְׁךָ
וּבְכָל-מְאֹדֶךָ: וְהָיוּ הַדְּבָרִים הָאֵלֶּה אֲשֶׁר אָנֹכִי מְצַוְּךָ
הַיּוֹם עַל-לְבָבֶךָ: וְשִׁנַּנְתָּם לְבָנֶיךָ וְדִבַּרְתָּ בָּם בְּשִׁבְתְּךָ
בְּבֵיתֶךָ וּבְלֶכְתְּךָ בַדֶּרֶךְ וּבְשָׁכְבְּךָ וּבְקוּמֶךָ: וּקְשַׁרְתָּם
לְאוֹת עַל-יָדֶךָ וְהָיוּ לְטֹטָפֹת בֵּין עֵינֶיךָ: וּכְתַבְתָּם
עַל-מְזֻזוֹת בֵּיתֶךָ וּבִשְׁעָרֶיךָ.

V'ahavta et Adonai Elohecha b'chol-l'vav'cha uv'chol-nafsh'cha uv'chol-m'odecha. V'hayu had'varim ha'eileh asher anochi m'tzavcha hayom al-l'vavecha. V'shinantam l'vanecha v'dibarta bam b'shivt'cha b'veitecha uv'lecht'cha vaderech uv'shochb'cha uv'kumecha. Uk'shartam l'ot al-yadecha v'hayu l'totafot bein einecha. Uch'tavtam al-m'zuzot beitecha uvish'arecha.

Love Adonai your God with all your heart, with all your soul, and with all your strength. Keep these words that I command you today in your heart. Teach them to your children. Speak about them when you sit in your home, when you walk on your way, when you go to sleep, and when you wake up. Bind them as a sign upon your hand and between your eyes. Write them on the doorposts of your house and on your gates. (Deuteronomy 6:4-9)

Mi Chamochah · מִי כָמֹכָה

מִי כָמֹכָה בָּאֵלִם יְיָ, מִי כָמֹכָה נֶאְדָּר בַּקֹּדֶשׁ,
נוֹרָא תְהִלֹּת, עֹשֵׂה פֶלֶא?

Mi chamochah ba'eilim Adonai, mi kamochah nedar bakodesh,
Nora t'hilot, oseih fele?

Who is like You, Adonai? Who is like You,
Holy and awesome, doing wonders?

שִׁירָה חֲדָשָׁה שִׁבְּחוּ גְאוּלִים
לְשִׁמְךָ עַל שְׂפַת הַיָּם,
יַחַד כֻּלָּם הוֹדוּ וְהִמְלִיכוּ וְאָמְרוּ:
יְיָ יִמְלֹךְ לְעוֹלָם וָעֶד.

Shirah chadashah shib'chu g'ulim l'shimcha al s'fat hayam, yachad
kulam hodu v'himlichu v'am'ru: Adonai yimloch l'olam va'ed.

Standing at the edge of the sea, the children of Israel sang a new
song before You: Adonai will rule always and forever!

צוּר יִשְׂרָאֵל, קוּמָה בְּעֶזְרַת יִשְׂרָאֵל,
וּפְדֵה כִנְאֻמֶךָ יְהוּדָה וְיִשְׂרָאֵל.
גָּאֲלֵנוּ יְיָ צְבָאוֹת שְׁמוֹ, קְדוֹשׁ יִשְׂרָאֵל.
בָּרוּךְ אַתָּה יְיָ, גָּאַל יִשְׂרָאֵל.

Tzur Yisrael, kumah b'ezrat Yisrael, ufdeih chinumecha Y'hudah
v'Yisrael. Go'aleinu Adonai Tz'va'ot sh'mo, k'dosh Yisrael. Baruch
Atah Adonai, ga'al Yisrael.

God, Rock of Israel, help us as You have helped our ancestors before
us. Praised are You, God, who saves the people Israel.

עֲמִידָה ✒ Amidah

אֲדֹנָי שְׂפָתַי תִּפְתָּח וּפִי יַגִּיד תְּהִלָּתֶךָ.

Adonai s'fatai tiftach ufi yagid t'hilatecha.

Adonai, open up my lips and my mouth will declare Your glory.

בָּרוּךְ אַתָּה יְיָ אֱלֹהֵינוּ וֵאלֹהֵי אֲבוֹתֵינוּ, אֱלֹהֵי אַבְרָהָם,
אֱלֹהֵי יִצְחָק, וֵאלֹהֵי יַעֲקֹב, אֱלֹהֵי שָׂרָה, אֱלֹהֵי רִבְקָה,
אֱלֹהֵי רָחֵל, וֵאלֹהֵי לֵאָה.

Baruch Atah Adonai Eloheinu v'Eilohei avoteinu, Elohei Avraham,
Elohei Yitzchak, v'Eilohei Ya'akov, Elohei Sarah, Elohei Rivkah, Elohei
Rachel, v'Eilohei Le'ah.

Praised are You God, God of our ancestors, the God of Abraham, the
God of Isaac, and the God of Jacob, the God of Sarah, the God of
Rebecca, the God of Rachel, and the God of Leah.

הָאֵל הַגָּדוֹל הַגִּבּוֹר וְהַנּוֹרָא, אֵל עֶלְיוֹן, גּוֹמֵל חֲסָדִים
טוֹבִים, וְקֹנֵה הַכֹּל, וְזוֹכֵר חַסְדֵי אָבוֹת, וּמֵבִיא גוֹאֵל
לִבְנֵי בְנֵיהֶם, לְמַעַן שְׁמוֹ בְּאַהֲבָה.

HaEil hagadol hagibor v'hanora, Eil elyon, gomeil chasadim tovim,
v'koneih hakol, v'zocheir chasdei avot, umeivi go'eil livnei v'neihem,
l'ma'an sh'mo b'ahavah.

Great, mighty, awesome God, who shows loving-kindness and
creates everything. You remember the goodness of our ancestors.
You care for us with love, as You will care for our children's children
and all generations to follow.

מֶלֶךְ עוֹזֵר וּמוֹשִׁיעַ וּמָגֵן. בָּרוּךְ אַתָּה יְיָ, מָגֵן אַבְרָהָם
וּפוֹקֵד שָׂרָה.

Melech ozeir umoshi'a umagein. Baruch Atah Adonai, magein
Avraham ufokeid Sarah.

God helps, saves, and shields. Praised are You, God, Abraham's
Shield and Sarah's Protector.

אַתָּה גִבּוֹר לְעוֹלָם אֲדֹנָי, מְחַיֵּה מֵתִים אַתָּה, רַב
לְהוֹשִׁיעַ.

Atah gibor l'olam Adonai, m'chayeih meitim Atah, rav l'hoshi'a.

God gives life to everything, God is mighty.

In winter (between Sh'mini Atzeret and Pesach)

מַשִּׁיב הָרוּחַ וּמוֹרִיד הַגָּשֶׁם.

Mashiv haru'ach umorid hagashem.

You cause the wind to blow and the rain to fall.

מְכַלְכֵּל חַיִּים בְּחֶסֶד, מְחַיֵּה מֵתִים בְּרַחֲמִים רַבִּים,
סוֹמֵךְ נוֹפְלִים, וְרוֹפֵא חוֹלִים, וּמַתִּיר אֲסוּרִים, וּמְקַיֵּם
אֱמוּנָתוֹ לִישֵׁנֵי עָפָר, מִי כָמוֹךְ בַּעַל גְּבוּרוֹת וּמִי דוֹמֶה
לָךְ, מֶלֶךְ מֵמִית וּמְחַיֶּה וּמַצְמִיחַ יְשׁוּעָה. וְנֶאֱמָן אַתָּה
לְהַחֲיוֹת מֵתִים. בָּרוּךְ אַתָּה יְיָ, מְחַיֵּה הַמֵּתִים.

*M'chalkeil chayim b'chesed, m'chayeih meitim b'rachamim rabim,
someich noflim, v'rofei cholim, umatir asurim, um'kayeim emunato
lisheinei afar, mi chamocha ba'al g'vurot umi domeh lach,
Melech meimit um'chayeh umatzmi'ach y'shu'ah. V'ne'eman Atah
l'hachayot meitim. Baruch Atah Adonai, m'chayeih hameitim.*

You fill our lives with loving-kindness. You give life to all, support us
when we fall, heal the sick, free the bound, and keep faith with those
who sleep in the dust. Who is like You, Adonai, who takes care of us?
Praised are You, God, who gives life to everything.

קְדוּשָׁה ↜ K'dushah

נְקַדֵּשׁ אֶת שִׁמְךָ בָּעוֹלָם, כְּשֵׁם שֶׁמַּקְדִּישִׁים אוֹתוֹ בִּשְׁמֵי
מָרוֹם, כַּכָּתוּב עַל יַד נְבִיאֶךָ, וְקָרָא זֶה אֶל זֶה וְאָמַר:

N'kadeish et shimcha ba'olam, k'sheim shemakdishim oto bishmei marom, kakatuv al yad n'vi'echa, v'kara zeh el zeh v'amar:

We make God's name holy on earth as the angels make God's name holy in heaven:

קָדוֹשׁ, קָדוֹשׁ, קָדוֹשׁ, יְיָ צְבָאוֹת, מְלֹא כָל הָאָרֶץ כְּבוֹדוֹ.

Kadosh, kadosh, kadosh, Adonai tz'va'ot, m'lo chol ha'aretz k'vodo.

Holy, Holy, Holy is God. All the world is filled with God's glory.

בָּרוּךְ כְּבוֹד יְיָ מִמְּקוֹמוֹ.

Baruch k'vod Adonai mim'komo.

Praised is God's glory.

יִמְלֹךְ יְיָ לְעוֹלָם, אֱלֹהַיִךְ צִיּוֹן, לְדֹר וָדֹר, הַלְלוּיָהּ.

Yimloch Adonai l'olam, Elohayich Tziyon, l'dor vador, hal'luyah.

God will rule forever and ever, Halleluyah!

Silent Prayer ❧ תְּפִילָה בְּלַחַשׁ

We take a moment to whisper our personal prayers to God.

Oseh Shalom ❧ עוֹשֶׂה שָׁלוֹם

עוֹשֶׂה שָׁלוֹם בִּמְרוֹמָיו,
הוּא יַעֲשֶׂה שָׁלוֹם עָלֵינוּ,
וְעַל כָּל יִשְׂרָאֵל,
וְאִמְרוּ אָמֵן.

Oseh shalom bimromav,
Hu ya'aseh shalom aleinu,
V'al kol Yisraeil,
V'imru amen.

May God who makes peace in heaven,
Make peace for us,
And for all Israel,
And for all people on earth,
And let us say: Amen.

הוֹצָאַת סֵפֶר תּוֹרָה ⟵ Taking Out the Torah

וַיְהִי בִּנְסֹעַ הָאָרֹן וַיֹּאמֶר מֹשֶׁה: קוּמָה, יְיָ, וְיָפֻצוּ אֹיְבֶיךָ,
וְיָנֻסוּ מְשַׂנְאֶיךָ מִפָּנֶיךָ. כִּי מִצִּיּוֹן תֵּצֵא תוֹרָה, וּדְבַר יְיָ
מִירוּשָׁלָיִם. בָּרוּךְ שֶׁנָּתַן תּוֹרָה לְעַמּוֹ יִשְׂרָאֵל בִּקְדֻשָּׁתוֹ.

*Va'y'hi binso'a ha'aron vayomer Moshe: kumah Adonai, v'yafutzu
oivecha, v'yanusu m'sanecha mipanecha. Ki miTziyon teitzei Torah,
ud'var Adonai miY'rushalayim. Baruch shenatan Torah l'amo Yisrael
bik'dushato.*

When the ark was carried forward, Moses would call to God and say:
"Arise, Adonai, and may Your enemies scatter!" Torah will come from
Zion, and the word of God from Jerusalem. Praised is God who gave
Torah to the people Israel in holiness.

Reader, then Congregation:

שְׁמַע יִשְׂרָאֵל, יְיָ אֱלֹהֵינוּ, יְיָ אֶחָד.

Sh'ma Yisrael, Adonai Eloheinu, Adonai Echad.

Hear O Israel, Adonai is our God, Adonai is One.

Reader, then Congregation:

אֶחָד אֱלֹהֵינוּ, גָּדוֹל אֲדוֹנֵנוּ, קָדוֹשׁ שְׁמוֹ.

Echad Eloheinu, gadol Adoneinu, kadosh sh'mo.

One is our God, great is our God, God's name is holy.

Reader:

גַּדְּלוּ לַיְיָ אִתִּי, וּנְרוֹמְמָה שְׁמוֹ יַחְדָּו.

Gad'lu l'Adonai iti, un'rom'mah sh'mo yachdav.

Praise Adonai's name with me; let us sing to God together.

Torah Reading ❧ קְרִיאַת הַתּוֹרָה

Before Reading from the Torah

The person honored with an aliyah recites:

בָּרְכוּ אֶת יְיָ הַמְבֹרָךְ!

Bar'chu et Adonai ham'vorach!

Praise God, the One who is blessed!

Congregation, then honoree repeats:

בָּרוּךְ יְיָ הַמְבֹרָךְ לְעוֹלָם וָעֶד!

Baruch Adonai ham'vorach l'olam va'ed!

Praised is God, the One who is blessed always and forever!

Honoree:

בָּרוּךְ אַתָּה יְיָ אֱלֹהֵינוּ מֶלֶךְ הָעוֹלָם, אֲשֶׁר בָּחַר בָּנוּ מִכָּל הָעַמִּים וְנָתַן לָנוּ אֶת תּוֹרָתוֹ. בָּרוּךְ אַתָּה יְיָ, נוֹתֵן הַתּוֹרָה.

Baruch Atah Adonai Eloheinu Melech ha'olam, asher bachar banu mikol ha'amim v'natan lanu et Torato. Baruch Atah Adonai, notein haTorah.

Praised are You, Adonai our God, Ruler of the universe, who has made us unique in giving us the Torah. Praised are You, God, who gives us the Torah.

After Reading from the Torah

Honoree:

בָּרוּךְ אַתָּה יְיָ אֱלֹהֵינוּ מֶלֶךְ הָעוֹלָם, אֲשֶׁר נָתַן לָנוּ תּוֹרַת אֱמֶת, וְחַיֵּי עוֹלָם נָטַע בְּתוֹכֵנוּ. בָּרוּךְ אַתָּה יְיָ, נוֹתֵן הַתּוֹרָה.

Baruch Atah Adonai Eloheinu Melech ha'olam, asher natan lanu Torat emet, v'chayei olam nata b'tocheinu. Baruch Atah Adonai, notein haTorah.

Praised are You, Adonai our God, Ruler of the universe, who has given us a Torah of truth, placing within us eternal life. Praised are You, God, who gives the Torah.

הַכְנָסַת סֵפֶר תּוֹרָה ⟿ Putting Away the Torah

וְזֹאת הַתּוֹרָה אֲשֶׁר שָׂם משֶׁה
לִפְנֵי בְּנֵי יִשְׂרָאֵל, עַל פִּי יְיָ בְּיַד משֶׁה.

V'zot haTorah asher sam Moshe lifnei b'nei Yisrael, al pi Adonai b'yad Moshe.

This is the Torah that Moses placed before the children of Israel, according to the will of God.

עֵץ חַיִּים הִיא ⟿ A Tree of Life

עֵץ חַיִּים הִיא לַמַּחֲזִיקִים בָּה, וְתֹמְכֶיהָ מְאֻשָּׁר.

Eitz chayim hi lamachazikim bah, v'tom'cheha m'ushar.

The Torah is a tree of life to those who hold fast to it, and all those who support it are happy.

דְּרָכֶיהָ דַרְכֵי נֹעַם, וְכָל נְתִיבוֹתֶיהָ שָׁלוֹם.
הֲשִׁיבֵנוּ יְיָ אֵלֶיךָ וְנָשׁוּבָה, חַדֵּשׁ יָמֵינוּ כְּקֶדֶם.

D'racheha darchei no'am, v'chol n'tivoteha shalom.
Hashiveinu Adonai eilecha v'nashuvah, chadeish yameinu k'kedem.

The ways of the Torah are pleasant;
The path of the Torah is peace.
Help us turn to You, Adonai, and we will return;
Restore us as in days of old.

עָלֵינוּ ⇐ Aleinu

עָלֵינוּ לְשַׁבֵּחַ לַאֲדוֹן הַכֹּל, לָתֵת גְּדֻלָּה לְיוֹצֵר בְּרֵאשִׁית,
שֶׁלֹּא עָשָׂנוּ כְּגוֹיֵי הָאֲרָצוֹת, וְלֹא שָׂמָנוּ כְּמִשְׁפְּחוֹת הָאֲדָמָה,
שֶׁלֹּא שָׂם חֶלְקֵנוּ כָּהֶם, וְגוֹרָלֵנוּ כְּכָל הֲמוֹנָם. וַאֲנַחְנוּ כּוֹרְעִים
וּמִשְׁתַּחֲוִים וּמוֹדִים, לִפְנֵי מֶלֶךְ מַלְכֵי הַמְּלָכִים, הַקָּדוֹשׁ
בָּרוּךְ הוּא.

Aleinu l'shabei'ach la'Adon hakol, lateit g'dulah l'yotzeir b'reisheet, shelo asanu k'goyei ha'aratzot, v'lo samanu k'mishp'chot ha'adamah, shelo sam chelkeinu kahem, v'goraleinu k'chol hamonam. Va'anachnu kor'im umishtachavim umodim, lifnei Melech malchei ham'lachim, hakadosh baruch Hu.

It is our special responsibility to praise God, the Creator of all. God made us unique among the nations and the families on earth. We bow and give thanks to God, the ruler of all rulers.

שֶׁהוּא נוֹטֶה שָׁמַיִם וְיֹסֵד אָרֶץ, וּמוֹשַׁב יְקָרוֹ בַּשָּׁמַיִם מִמַּעַל,
וּשְׁכִינַת עֻזּוֹ בְּגָבְהֵי מְרוֹמִים, הוּא אֱלֹהֵינוּ אֵין עוֹד. אֱמֶת
מַלְכֵּנוּ, אֶפֶס זוּלָתוֹ, כַּכָּתוּב בְּתוֹרָתוֹ: וְיָדַעְתָּ הַיּוֹם וַהֲשֵׁבֹתָ
אֶל לְבָבֶךָ, כִּי יְיָ הוּא הָאֱלֹהִים בַּשָּׁמַיִם מִמַּעַל, וְעַל הָאָרֶץ
מִתַּחַת, אֵין עוֹד.

SheHu noteh shamayim v'yoseid aretz, umoshav y'karo bashamayim mima'al, ush'chinat uzo b'govhei m'romim, Hu Eloheinu ein od. Emet Malkeinu, efes zulato, kakatuv b'Torato: V'yadata hayom vahasheivota el l'vavecha, ki Adonai Hu ha'Elohim bashamayim mima'al, v'al ha'aretz mitachat, ein od.

God created heaven and earth. Adonai is our God; there is no other.

כַּכָּתוּב בְּתוֹרָתֶךָ, יְיָ יִמְלֹךְ לְעֹלָם וָעֶד. וְנֶאֱמַר, וְהָיָה יְיָ לְמֶלֶךְ
עַל כָּל הָאָרֶץ, בַּיּוֹם הַהוּא יִהְיֶה יְיָ אֶחָד, וּשְׁמוֹ אֶחָד.

Kakatuv b'Toratecha, Adonai yimloch l'olam va'ed. V'ne'emar, v'hayah Adonai l'melech al kol ha'aretz, bayom hahu yih'yeh Adonai echad, ushmo echad.

As it is written in Your Torah: God will rule forever and always. God will be one, and the name of God will be one.

Mourner's Kaddish ⇜ קַדִּישׁ יָתוֹם

We remember those whom we have loved but who are no longer
with us on earth. We are thankful to God for our time with them and
for our memories of them.

יִתְגַּדַּל וְיִתְקַדַּשׁ שְׁמֵהּ רַבָּא. בְּעָלְמָא דִּי בְרָא כִרְעוּתֵהּ,
וְיַמְלִיךְ מַלְכוּתֵהּ בְּחַיֵּיכוֹן וּבְיוֹמֵיכוֹן וּבְחַיֵּי דְכָל בֵּית
יִשְׂרָאֵל, בַּעֲגָלָא וּבִזְמַן קָרִיב, וְאִמְרוּ אָמֵן.

*Yitgadal v'yitkadash sh'meih raba. B'alma di v'ra chiruteih,
v'yamlich malchuteih b'chayeichon uv'yomeichon uv'chayei d'chol
beit Yisrael, ba'agala uvizman kariv, v'imru amen.*

יְהֵא שְׁמֵהּ רַבָּא מְבָרַךְ לְעָלַם וּלְעָלְמֵי עָלְמַיָּא.

Y'hei sh'meih raba m'varach l'alam ul'al'mei al'maya.

יִתְבָּרַךְ וְיִשְׁתַּבַּח וְיִתְפָּאַר וְיִתְרוֹמַם וְיִתְנַשֵּׂא וְיִתְהַדָּר
וְיִתְעַלֶּה וְיִתְהַלָּל שְׁמֵהּ דְּקֻדְשָׁא בְּרִיךְ הוּא, לְעֵלָּא מִן כָּל
בִּרְכָתָא וְשִׁירָתָא תֻּשְׁבְּחָתָא וְנֶחֱמָתָא, דַּאֲמִירָן בְּעָלְמָא,
וְאִמְרוּ אָמֵן.

*Yitbarach v'yishtabach v'yitpa'ar v'yitromam v'yitnasei v'yithadar
v'yitaleh v'yit'halal sh'meih d'kud'sha b'rich Hu, l'eila min kol birchata
v'shirata tushb'chata v'nechemata, da'amiran b'alma, v'imru amen.*

יְהֵא שְׁלָמָא רַבָּא מִן שְׁמַיָּא, וְחַיִּים עָלֵינוּ וְעַל כָּל יִשְׂרָאֵל,
וְאִמְרוּ אָמֵן.

*Y'hei sh'lama raba min sh'maya, v'chayim aleinu v'al kol Yisrael,
v'imru amen.*

עֹשֶׂה שָׁלוֹם בִּמְרוֹמָיו, הוּא יַעֲשֶׂה שָׁלוֹם עָלֵינוּ וְעַל כָּל
יִשְׂרָאֵל, וְאִמְרוּ אָמֵן.

*Oseh shalom bimromav, Hu ya'aseh shalom aleinu v'al kol Yisrael,
v'imru amen.*

May their memory always be a blessing.

אֲדוֹן עוֹלָם ~ Adon Olam

בְּטֶרֶם כָּל יְצִיר נִבְרָא.   אֲדוֹן עוֹלָם אֲשֶׁר מָלַךְ,
אֲזַי מֶלֶךְ שְׁמוֹ נִקְרָא.   לְעֵת נַעֲשָׂה בְחֶפְצוֹ כֹּל,

Adon olam asher malach, b'terem kol y'tzir nivra.
L'eit na'asah v'cheftzo kol, azai Melech sh'mo nikra.

לְבַדּוֹ יִמְלוֹךְ נוֹרָא.   וְאַחֲרֵי כִּכְלוֹת הַכֹּל,
וְהוּא יִהְיֶה בְּתִפְאָרָה.   וְהוּא הָיָה וְהוּא הוֶֹה,

V'acharei kichlot hakol, l'vado yimloch nora.
V'Hu hayah v'Hu hoveh, v'Hu yihyeh b'tifarah.

לְהַמְשִׁיל לוֹ לְהַחְבִּירָה.   וְהוּא אֶחָד וְאֵין שֵׁנִי,
וְלוֹ הָעֹז וְהַמִּשְׂרָה.   בְּלִי רֵאשִׁית בְּלִי תַכְלִית,

V'hu echad v'ein sheini, l'hamshil lo l'hachbirah.
B'li reishit b'li tachlit, v'lo ha'oz v'hamisrah.

וְצוּר חֶבְלִי בְּעֵת צָרָה.   וְהוּא אֵלִי וְחַי גֹּאֲלִי,
מְנָת כּוֹסִי בְּיוֹם אֶקְרָא.   וְהוּא נִסִּי וּמָנוֹס לִי,

V'Hu Eili v'chai go'ali, v'tzur chevli b'eit tzarah.
V'Hu nisi umanos li, m'nat kosi b'yom ekra.

בְּעֵת אִישָׁן וְאָעִירָה.   בְּיָדוֹ אַפְקִיד רוּחִי,
יְיָ לִי וְלֹא אִירָא.   וְעִם רוּחִי גְּוִיָּתִי,

B'yado afkid ruchi, b'eit ishan v'a'irah.
V'im ruchi g'viyati, Adonai li v'lo ira.

God is always with us—yesterday, today, and tomorrow; here, there, and everywhere.

Kiddush ❧ קִדּוּשׁ

וְשָׁמְרוּ בְנֵי יִשְׂרָאֵל אֶת הַשַּׁבָּת, לַעֲשׂוֹת אֶת הַשַּׁבָּת לְדֹרֹתָם בְּרִית עוֹלָם. בֵּינִי וּבֵין בְּנֵי יִשְׂרָאֵל אוֹת הִיא לְעֹלָם, כִּי שֵׁשֶׁת יָמִים עָשָׂה יְיָ אֶת הַשָּׁמַיִם וְאֶת הָאָרֶץ, וּבַיּוֹם הַשְּׁבִיעִי שָׁבַת וַיִּנָּפַשׁ.

V'sham'ru v'nei Yisrael et haShabbat, la'asot et haShabbat l'dorotam b'rit olam. Beini uvein b'nei Yisrael ot hi l'olam, ki sheishet yamim asah Adonai et hashamayim v'et ha'aretz, uvayom hash'vi'i shavat vayinafash.

The people Israel will keep Shabbat forever. It is a sign between Me and the people Israel that in six days God created the heavens and the earth, and on the seventh day, God rested.

בָּרוּךְ אַתָּה יְיָ אֱלֹהֵינוּ מֶלֶךְ הָעוֹלָם, בּוֹרֵא פְּרִי הַגָּפֶן.

Baruch Atah Adonai Eloheinu Melech ha'olam, borei p'ri hagafen.

Praised are You, Adonai our God, Ruler of the universe, Creator of the fruit of the vine.

Hamotzi ❧ הַמּוֹצִיא

בָּרוּךְ אַתָּה יְיָ אֱלֹהֵינוּ מֶלֶךְ הָעוֹלָם, הַמּוֹצִיא לֶחֶם מִן הָאָרֶץ.

Baruch Atah Adonai Eloheinu Melech ha'olam, hamotzi lechem min ha'aretz.

Praised are You, Adonai our God, Ruler of the universe, who brings forth bread from the earth.